BITCOIN

How To Get Started With Bitcoin

Tim Mathis

© **Copyright 2017 by Tim Mathis**
- All rights reserved.

This document is geared towards providing exact and reliable information in regards to the topic and issue covered. The publication is sold with the idea that the publisher is not required to render accounting, officially permitted, or otherwise, qualified services. If advice is necessary, legal or professional, a practiced individual in the profession should be ordered.

- From a Declaration of Principles which was accepted and approved equally by a Committee of the American Bar Association and a Committee of Publishers and Associations.

In no way is it legal to reproduce, duplicate, or transmit any part of this document in either electronic means or in printed format. Recording of this publication is strictly prohibited and any storage of this document is not allowed unless with written permission from the publisher. All rights reserved.

The information provided herein is stated to be truthful and consistent, in that any liability, in terms of inattention or otherwise, by any usage or abuse of any policies, processes, or directions contained within is the solitary and utter responsibility of the recipient reader. Under no circumstances will any legal responsibility or blame be held against the publisher for any reparation, damages, or monetary loss due to the information herein, either directly or indirectly.

Respective authors own all copyrights not held by the publisher.

The information herein is offered for informational purposes solely, and is universal as so. The presentation of the information is without contract or any type of guarantee assurance.

The trademarks that are used are without any consent, and the publication of the trademark is without permission or backing by the trademark owner. All trademarks and brands within this book are for clarifying purposes only and are the owned by the owners themselves, not affiliated with this document.

Table of Contents

Introduction 1

Chapter 1 – Setting up a Wallet 3

   A brief history of money 4

   Buying your first bitcoin in 15 minutes 5
      Signing up for a wallet – five minutes 7
      Adding a funding source – ten minutes 8
      Buying Bitcoin – less than a minute 9
      Looking at your Bitcoin balance 9
      Explaining Bitcoin addresses 10

   Sending and receiving Bitcoins 12
      Sending Bitcoins 12
      Receiving Bitcoins 13

   Private keys and wallets 14

   Transactions and confirmations 15
      Transactions 16
      Confirmations 17

   Comparing Bitcoin wallets 19
      Online wallets 19

   Desktop wallets 20
      Mobile wallets 21
      Hardware wallets 22

Chapter 2 – Understanding the Blockchain 23

   The Genesis block 24

   Satoshi Nakamoto 25

- The White Paper 26
- The Blockchain 27
- Keys, transactions, and blocks 27
  - Creating a transaction 28
  - Digital signatures 29
  - Public key encryption 29
  - Signing a document 30
- Elliptic Curve Cryptography 31
  - Bitcoin addresses 31
  - Generating a Bitcoin address 32
  - Signing a transaction 33
- Decentralized network 34
  - Broadcasting the transaction 35
  - The Blockchain 36
  - Blocks 36
  - Forks 37
- The Bitcoin supply 39
  - Proof of work 40
  - Confirmation 40
  - Difficulty level 41
  - Mining 41
  - Solving a difficult problem 42
  - Transaction fees 43
- Network attacks 44
  - 51 percent attacks 44
  - Race attacks 45
  - Finney attacks 45
  - Alternative coins 45

Chapter 3 – The Mining Process 47

Digital gold 48

Bitcoin mining 49

Exploring the mining ecosystem 50
- Validating transactions 51
- Proof-of-Work 52
- SHA-256 53
- Scrypt 53
- Mining rewards 54
- Mining hardware 55
- Mining conditions 56
- Mining pools 57
- Mining shares 58
- Fees and Payout 58
- Cloud mining 59
- Estimating profitability 59
- Hardware efficiency 60
- Factoring in the difficulty level 60
- Selecting a currency 62
- Exchange rates 62

Setting up a mining client 63
- Requirements 63

Connecting to a mining pool 67
- The payout method 67
- The pool fees 68
- The pool speed 68
- Additional features 68
- Avoiding large pools 69

Running the client 69

Chapters 4 – Is it Worth Investing in Bitcoins 71

Advantages of Bitcoin 72

Disadvantages of Bitcoin 73

Conclusion 77

The future of finance 77

Introduction

The emergence of digital currency has caused some disruption in the financial world, especially relating to the future of entire economies. To the average person, the whole idea of a virtual currency existing only over the internet seems implausible. After all, if something doesn't exist in the form of physical coins or notes, how can it possibly be considered real currency?

What most people overlook is the money they spend from their own regular banking accounts on a daily basis also only exists on their bank's computer systems. Your salary might be credited directly into your bank, where the figure available is shown as a set of digital numbers. Likewise, the money you borrow from your bank for a mortgage or personal loan is actually a set of digital figures transacted from your account to the seller's account on a virtual system.

Believe it or not, this type of 'virtual' banking has been prevailing since the rapid rise of the fractional banking system several centuries ago. Think about it: does every bank in the world actually carry the amount of cash required to pay all of its depositors if they all stormed in on the same day and demanded their money?

BITCOIN

Of course not. Banks carry only a small percentage of the actual amounts required for withdrawals. However, banks can lend money based on funds created using the virtual fractional banking system.

As the fractional banking system has been around for a few centuries now, nobody really blinks an eye at the idea of virtual currency in those terms.

When you introduce them to the idea of virtual digital currency, a new level of skepticism emerges. In recent decades, the idea of paying for items using digital payment processors, such as Paypal, has become more widely accepted by many people.

When you transact via an online payment processor, the figures you enter exist only as digital currencies. If you sell an item online via an e-commerce site, such as eBay, the buyer deposits digital currency into your Paypal account. You are then able to use that digital currency to purchase other items elsewhere. The virtual amounts of money only ever become real when you withdraw those amounts into your own bank account and then access them via a local ATM. Only then does the money shift from virtual to become real, physical currency.

Thanks for downloading this book. It's my firm belief that it will provide you with all the answers to your questions

Chapter 1:

Setting up a Wallet

Bitcoin's potential is quickly becoming apparent in the rapidly changing world of Internet finance. In just a few short years since its launch, we have seen an explosion of interest in this new, and somewhat mysterious, Internet money.

Several questions quickly come to mind:

How does it work?

Where does it come from?

How do I buy it?

In this chapter, we will illustrate, in simple terms, most of what anyone new to Bitcoin will need to know to start. We will start by covering the following core topics:

1. Buying your first bitcoin, in 15 minutes

2. Explaining Bitcoin addresses

3. Sending and receiving

4. Private keys and wallets

5. Transactions and confirmations
6. Comparing Bitcoin wallets

A brief history of money

Humans have been trading various forms of money for thousands of years. Many types of precious objects, acting as medium of exchange, have been used. In the early ages, we traded grain, cattle, shells, and gems for other goods and services.

This type of money, which we can touch and see, can be considered Physical Money.

As civilization progressed, so did our political systems. Eventually, sparse tribes and villages consolidated into kingdoms, states, and empires. Through the transformation, we saw our money shift into Political Money; money that's governed and issued by a central body such as the King, Emperor or, as in today's society, a Central Bank. State issued coins, bills, and notes, as well as taxation, regulation, and monetary policy—all emerged from this shift.

Today, Internet technology connects us directly to each other, opening a vast range of possibilities. By dissolving pre-existing physical and political boundaries, for the first time in history, the entire planet has access to the same information. This level of access is guaranteed by the Internet's decentralized design. Without a centralized hub, there is no single point of failure or control.

Chapter 1 – Setting up a Wallet

Satoshi Nakamoto, the creator of Bitcoin, leveraged this powerful network to implement a peer-to-peer (P2P) system for exchanging virtual cash. Built on a decentralized design and protected by powerful cryptography, this new type of money is no longer physical, yet resilient against corruption and manipulation.

No single group of individuals, including governments, banks, and corporations, control Bitcoin because all the peers are equal actors, participating in the same protocol. Its monetary policy is defined and self-regulated by its open network of computers. Thus, with Bitcoin, we're seeing the emergence of a new phase of money. This P2P money is called cryptographic money or simply Crypto-Currency.

We're going to start exploring the world of Bitcoin by purchasing a small amount.

Buying your first bitcoin in 15 minutes

Buying bitcoin is similar to buying foreign currencies. When an American lands in Paris, the first thing he/she may need to do is exchange dollars for Euros. While at the airport, it's likely he/she will be able to find a currency exchange. Just as there are many exchanges for exchanging government currencies, there are many exchanges for exchanging bitcoins.

Today there are markets for exchanging bitcoin with most of the world's major currencies. Most of them are online markets through which you can connect your bank account or credit card. There are some markets where the buyer and seller meet in person to exchange by hand. For the more technical users, private markets exist on chat forums where anonymous users trade with the other users based on their online reputation.

Of all the diverse ways to buy bitcoin, using a reputable online exchange may be the likely option for most users. Online exchanges generally operate similar to conventional online banking systems and are easy to set up.

We're going to buy 25 dollars' worth of bitcoin using a credit card with an online exchange called Circle. In 2013, Circle was launched by a team competent in technology and finance. Additionally, they are registered as a money transmitter with FinCEN, a US government agency responsible for safeguarding the financial system from illicit use. For US citizens, they offer an instant exchange with a user-friendly Wallet, service. To buy bitcoins with Circle, you'll need the following:

1. Valid photo ID
2. A US home or business address
3. A US bank account or credit card
4. An iOS or Android smartphone
5. 15 Minutes of free time

Buying and selling bitcoin on Circle is only available to users with a US address. As a registered money transmitter, Circle must follow standard banking practices such as Know Your Customer (KYC) and Anti-Money Laundering laws (AML). These are the requirements to accept bank transfers from the US banking system.

Chapter 1 – Setting up a Wallet

Most European and Canadian customers can use Coinbase for direct wire transfers. What's important to remember about Bitcoin is that the currency exists independently of any government's requirement for an individual's identity. Bitcoins can be exchanged for cash hand-to-hand, thus bypassing the registration process that we will describe in this chapter.

There are services such as local Bitcoins where the users can buy and sell Bitcoin through direct exchange with the other users. While it is safe to do so, some users may be at risk from local regulations. It is important to research the local currency laws before transacting through these services, especially with a large amount of cash.

Signing up for a wallet – five minutes

To begin the signup process, open http://circle.com in your web browser and follow the SIGN-UP links. You will be prompted to enter your first name, your last name, your Email address, and a password. After submitting your details, Circle will send you an e-mail verification. Simply follow the instructions provided. If you don't receive the email, check the spam folder of the email address you provided.

After verifying your email address, you'll be asked to enable two-factor authentication using your mobile phone. This security system uses a code sent via SMS or through Google Authenticator to allow access to your account and confirm irreversible actions, such as sending bitcoin. This helps make your account more secure by combining your password with something you physically hold, that is, your phone.

BITCOIN

Finally, Circle will prompt you to provide two security questions. In case you lose your password, these questions will be asked before you can reset it.

Adding a funding source – ten minutes

To purchase Bitcoin, Circle requires a funding source. You can link a US bank account or a credit card. For this purpose, we will choose the credit card option as it's the quickest to set up.

1. On the ACCOUNT page, which should show your balance as zero, click on the Add Funds button.

    A circle will prompt you to verify your mailing address along with your birth date and the last four digits of your social security number. This information is used to help verify your identification.

2. Next, Circle will ask you to install their mobile application (available for iOS or Android). Using their mobile app, you'll be prompted to take a picture of yourself and your photo ID. Ensure that you arrange for proper lighting so that the image clearly shows the details of each digit. Once submitted, a confirmation will be given within a few minutes.

3. If the app doesn't prompt you to verify your photo ID, you can manually upload the images. Open the mobile app under the Account table and click on the Settings icon. Under the Settings, click on Link Accounts. By following the instructions, you'll be prompted to upload the photos of your documents and credit card.

Chapter 1 – Setting up a Wallet

At any stage, if you're experiencing issues, Circle offers support through online messaging. It also has toll free phone support for urgent issues.

4. After your identification has been verified, you're ready to add your credit card as a funding source. Return to your Circle account page and click on Add Funds. A circle will prompt you to enter your credit card information and will save it for future use.

Buying Bitcoin – less than a minute

Once added, you're ready to buy Bitcoin! Simply enter a dollar amount ($25 for our example), and review the Bitcoin amount. You can preview and confirm any additional fees or charges below. Accepting the order will initiate an instant deposit to your online Bitcoin wallet.

Looking at your Bitcoin balance

On your Circle account page, you can find the exact Bitcoin balance under your dollar balance.

Also indicated on your account page, under the balance, is the current USD to BTC exchange rate for Circle. The exchange rate can vary between services, depending on the supply and demand.

Bitcoin amounts are usually noted with the abbreviation BTC. This is similar to other currencies, such as USD and EUR. There are a few other symbols accepted by the Bitcoin community.

BITCOIN

Bitcoin amounts can have up to eight digits of precision. While every Bitcoin wallet must account for each digit of precision, the minimum amount that you can send may vary. Circle's minimum sends amount is 0.00005460 BTC which is current with the amount proposed by the Bitcoin community.

Referring to the preceding table, you can write 0.44234 BTC as 442.34 mBTC. Some services and exchanges have adopted this format to make your account balance easier to read. Because amounts listed in whole numbers are easier to hold in one's mind, displaying the amounts in mBTC can be ideal. A cup of coffee at the time of this writing costs around **10mBTC**.

Note:

The smallest unit of bitcoin, 0.00000001 BTC, is called a Satoshi, named after the developer of Bitcoin, Satoshi Nakamoto.

Some wallets allow you to change the unit of bitcoin presented in the settings. This may make accounting and calculations easier, depending on your use case, especially if the exchange rate has many decimal places.

Explaining Bitcoin addresses

Similar to an email address, a Bitcoin address, or simply address, is used to receive and hold Bitcoin. While people typically have one primary email address, Bitcoin users have many addresses. They are created at no cost to your Bitcoin wallet each time you request to receive money. Anyone with access to a Bitcoin wallet can create an unlimited number of addresses.

Chapter 1 – Setting up a Wallet

Bitcoin addresses usually have 26-35 characters and are case sensitive, as in the following example:

1MgErLiH1DuGMrd58fuL4CLQHc4VSboqKn

The address can contain numbers and letters, both uppercase and lowercase. To help reduce confusion, there is no capital O's, zeros 0's, lower case l's, and capital 'I's.' These characters are removed to reduce the errors made from writing with pen and paper, as often encountered in the past. The result is a format that is easy to share digitally and/or physically.

Bitcoin addresses have an error-checking code called a checksum. Computing the checksum of an address will detect if any single character is incorrect. This helps to prevent errors when sharing your address. Most wallets will validate and reject an invalid address. As an example, note the following two addresses:

- Valid Bitcoin address:

  1MgErLiH1DuGMrd58fuL4CLQHc4VSboqKn

- Invalid Bitcoin address:

  1MgErLiH1DuGMrd58fuL4CLQHc4VSboqKN

They both appear valid, yet the second address does not compute a valid checksum. They are nearly identical except for the uppercase N at the end of the second address.

Note:

Checksums have been used in finance for many years. All credit card numbers have a built-in checksum digit, specific to the issuing bank.

Your Bitcoin wallet will typically hold many Bitcoin addresses. It's important to know that a single Bitcoin address is not a wallet nor is it your account; rather, it's simply a way to receive money.

Sending and receiving Bitcoins

Your wallet's total spendable balance is a combination of the balances from all the Bitcoin addresses listed in the wallet. When spending Bitcoins, the wallet can combine the balances of multiple addresses into one transaction.

Sending Bitcoins

From your Circle account, simply click the SEND MONEY link from the menu above to access the send options. Circle offers two ways to send Bitcoin. You can either send it to a Bitcoin address or an email address.

If you are sending it to an email address, Circle will check to see if the address has a valid account registered to it and make an instant deposit into that user's wallet. If the receiver is not registered, an invitation will be sent with instructions on how to set up an account.

In the To field, simply enter the Bitcoin address or the email address of the user you'd like to pay. For the amount, you can specify either USD or BTC. If you enter an amount in USD, Circle will automatically calculate the exchange rate. Optionally, you can provide a memo to describe your transaction.

Continuing to the next step, Circle will prompt you to enter your two-factor authentication code. This code will be sent to your mobile phone. Using this two-factor authentication helps protect your wallet from unauthorized access.

Once submitted, your transaction will be recorded instantly.

For payments between two Circle users, the transaction will be confirmed immediately. Circle maintains an internal ledger and will record the transaction on the Bitcoin network.

For payments sent to a Bitcoin address, there will be a short period before the transaction is confirmed and accepted by the network. This takes about 10 minutes, but it can vary depending on the network's computing power.

You can review all your payments by clicking TRANSACTIONS from the main menu.

Receiving Bitcoins

Circle provides two ways to receive Bitcoin. Similar to sending Bitcoin, you can send a request via email or share your Bitcoin address.

To start, click the REQUEST MONEY link from the main menu above. You'll be prompted to create a request:

BITCOIN

If you submit an email address, the recipient will receive an email providing them with instructions on how to pay. They will be given the following options:

- Sign into their Circle account and pay
- Open a new Circle account, fund it, and pay
- Pay with another service using a Bitcoin address

If you select the option to create an address and QR code, Circle will generate a new Bitcoin address for you and present a QR code to scan. You can either copy/paste the address and share it with the sender, or allow them to scan the QR using a mobile device.

Private keys and wallets

While Bitcoin addresses appear to be a string of random numbers, they are computed from a private key. Private keys are long strings of random characters generated by your Bitcoin wallet software. There can only be one address generated from your private key; thus your private key is both the seed and password to your Bitcoin address.

Bitcoin private keys contain 51 characters and start with a 5, such as in the following example:

5Jd54v5mVLvyRsjDGTFbTZFGvwLosYKayRosbLYMxZFBLfEpCS7

Similar to your pocket wallet with credit cards, your Bitcoin wallet is a collection of addresses and private keys. Each address is used to receive and hold Bitcoin.

While most Bitcoin software holding your Bitcoin are called wallets, they are technically keychains. Keychains are designed to manage and protect your Bitcoin keys. The term wallet is a convention carried over from Bitcoin legacy software.

Reputable online wallets take the necessary precautions to protect your private keys. Most online wallets use a technique called cold storage. Holding private keys in cold storage means that your keys are physically stored offline in a vault. Access to the vault is required to interact with the keys.

Additionally, multi-signature addresses are used to protect the coins in cold storage. Typically, an address will require one key to transfer its Bitcoins. Multi-signature addresses usually require two or more keys to sign a transfer. With cold storage, there will often be a two of three requirements so that no one employee has full access to the funds.

Private keys are generated from large amounts of random data, called entropy in computer science, and are very difficult to crack. With all the computing power available today, it is not possible to find the private key of a Bitcoin address using brute force methods. Even if computing power were to exponentially increase to the point where that's possible, the Bitcoin software can be upgraded to include new cryptographic methods to match.

Transactions and confirmations

The Bitcoin network is essentially a public ledger that's able to record and validate millions of transactions. Transactions validated by the network are irreversible and impossible to change or alter. In this section, we're going to look at two core aspects of the network: transactions and confirmations.

Transactions

A Bitcoin transaction is a record of a transfer between two or more bitcoin addresses. Similar to a credit or debit on your bank statement, the transaction records the sender, the receiver, and a date/time stamp.

All Bitcoin transactions are publicly accessible. However, the user's identity is never stored. Similar to a Swiss bank account, only their public addresses are recorded. This makes it difficult to trace the address back to its owner. Therefore, we say that Bitcoin is pseudonymous.

More flexible than a simple bank transfer, a Bitcoin transaction can withdraw from multiple addresses to pay a list of addresses. The transaction records every address used and must account for the full balance. Any unspent Bitcoin must be sent back to a "change address." It works like paying for an item that costs 12 dollars with two 10 dollar bills. The merchant accepts the two bills and returns 8 dollars in change.

We then send 4BTC to the receiver. To account for the full balance, the transaction returns 1BTC to our change address. After the transaction, the two funding addresses will contain 0BTC each.

The change address is optional as we can reuse an existing Bitcoin address. However, most wallets create a new address as it's recommended to increase your privacy.

Before sending a transaction to the Bitcoin network for confirmation, it must be signed with the private keys of the input addresses listed. Similar to your bank requiring your signature on a check, the Bitcoin network requires you to sign your transaction before confirming it.

Bitcoin uses a digital signature to sign your transaction. The signature can only be generated by the holder of the private key.

The digital signature is used by the network to verify that the transaction was created by someone who has access to the private key. Without this verification, the transaction would be rejected from the public ledger.

The process of computing the digital signature is handled automatically by your Bitcoin wallet. The digitally signed transaction is now ready for confirmation by the network. We will discuss digital signatures in detail in the next chapter: Understanding the Blockchain.

Confirmations

After it's digitally signed, the transaction is broadcasted to the Bitcoin network and reviewed by many nodes on the network. Each node is essentially a computer with a copy of the ledger, with access to all the transactions since the beginning. The node's job is to listen for new transactions and relay them to the other nodes on the network.

Some nodes serve as miners. Miners perform computational work to ensure that each transaction is valid; that it does not double the transaction or spend more than the available balance. Each miner must then prove the results to the other miners. Any discrepancies will cause the network to reject a miner's results.

This process is what makes the Bitcoin network both resilient and trustworthy. The larger the network of miners with consensus, the more we can trust the validity of the ledger. This is how Atoshi was able to design a network for exchanging virtual cash without a single point of control or failure.

Unconfirmed transactions start with zero confirmations. When a miner's work is accepted by the network, the number of confirmations for each transaction is incremented by one. Confirmations are generally accepted every 10 minutes but can vary depending on the various computational aspects of the network.

As more miners confirm the results of the previous miners, the number of confirmations for your transaction continues to increase. After some time, your transaction can have hundreds or even thousands of confirmations. With such a large number of confirmations, you can be assured that your transaction cannot be reversed.

The Bitcoin network is a very powerful network, especially when there is a large number of miners working together to validate and confirm the transactions on a public ledger. The entire ledger is copied by new miners joining the network. Transactions confirmed by an increasing number of miners results in more trust in the network. This design creates redundancy to guard against transaction fraud. Once a transaction is confirmed in the ledger, it cannot be deleted or changed.

Chapter 1 – Setting up a Wallet

Now that we have a basic understanding of how Bitcoin works, let's look at some wallet services and compare their differences.

Comparing Bitcoin wallets

We have been using Circle as an online wallet to help make the introduction to Bitcoin gentler and safer. Yet there are other options we can use for sending and receiving Bitcoin. Each option has its advantages and disadvantages. Let's briefly discuss them now.

Online wallets

Services such as Circle are called online wallets. Online wallets are web-based services that manage and store a small amount of your Bitcoins on a public web server. The rest are stored offline in a physical vault. They generally have the following characteristics:

- Available through a web browser or mobile application
- Create and store your private keys online
- Offer the option to send/receive via email address
- Have a built-in exchange to buy/sell bitcoin
- Offer quick and easy account signup
- Can be secured via two-factor authentication
- May offer insurance for loss of coins

BITCOIN

While these are nice features to offer the public, some of the more proficient users are not in favor of having an organization control their funds.

In the past, some exchanges have suffered security breaches. While some of the services were able to cover the losses, others were not solvent and were unable to reimburse its users. That resulted in many users losing their funds.

When choosing an online wallet, be sure to do your research on the company, the team, and its history.

Desktop wallets

For users who would like more control over their Bitcoin, desktop wallets may be a better choice than online wallets.

Desktop wallets are applications that run on your computer and connect directly to the Bitcoin network. Having the application installed locally gives the users full control of their Bitcoin wallet and their private keys.

Some desktop wallets, such as Bitcoin Core, download a full copy of the Bitcoin ledger to disk. This can require more than 10 gigabytes of local storage and can take a couple of days to download and verify.

More efficient desktop wallets, called lightweight clients, connect to an online copy of the ledger. This reduces the storage requirements and the set up time. In most cases, your wallet can be ready within a few minutes.

Chapter 1 – Setting up a Wallet

The risk of using a desktop wallet includes hardware failures, computer viruses, and unauthorized access. Before accepting any Bitcoin to your desktop wallet, you should be familiar with the backup and restore process, and you must ensure that your computer is safe from malicious attacks.

For more advanced users, many desktop wallets offer a console where they can interact with their wallet by issuing commands. Users can generate various kinds of transactions and directly manipulate their list of private keys and addresses.

Mobile wallets

Having access from your mobile phone is a practical way to carry and spend Bitcoins on the go. Most of the online services mentioned previously have applications available for download on the iPhone and Android app stores. Because the Bitcoin keys are stored and managed on servers, your account is protected by your username and password.

Tip:

To increase the security of Bitcoins stored on a mobile device, make sure to set up a PIN code for unlocking the phone.

It's also worth mentioning that there are independent mobile wallets that store access to the keys on the phone. Because storing the private keys on your phone can be risky in the event it's lost or stolen, the wallets offer a way to protect your Bitcoin with 24 words that are randomly chosen. You will be able to restore your wallet, if lost, using the passphrase.

BITCOIN

Hardware wallets

As one of the most secure options, hardware wallets store and encrypt your private keys on removable USB devices. Because the keys are never copied to your computer or made available online, it makes it extremely difficult to hack.

During set up, the hardware wallet will generate 24 random words, similar to the mobile wallets, as the password to your Bitcoin. Backing up your wallet is as simple as backing up the list of words. To restore your device, you simply provide the same set of words during set up.

The two commercially available hardware wallets are Ledger (https://www.ledgerwallet.com) and Trezor (www.bitcointrezor.com). They both plug into your USB port and include a user-friendly interface.

Chapter 2:

Understanding the Blockchain

Bitcoin's underlying transaction database is called the Blockchain. Its novel design, as a distributed ledger, allows it to function without any trusted central authority.

Understanding how it works is essential for integrating information systems with Bitcoin. In this chapter, you will be given a simplified explanation of the Blockchain's internal mechanisms. Building on the previous chapters, we'll cover the following subjects in more detail:

- Keys, transactions, and blocks
- Digital signatures
- Cryptographic hashes
- The Blockchain
- Nodes and miners
- Decentralized design
- Network attacks
- Alternative

The Genesis block

September 15th, 2008 marked a defining moment for the finance industry, as Lehman Brothers, at that time the fourth largest investment bank, filed for chapter 11 bankruptcy after massive losses in stock price and assets. The collapse marked the beginning of the Global Financial Crisis of 2008.

Shortly after, Bitcoin, a new type of virtual currency, was launched by an anonymous developer, or group of developers, under the name Satoshi Nakamoto. The software was built on a publicly-accessible transaction ledger that is distributed and validated by a network of independent nodes. More importantly, its design was powerfully resilient to attacks.

The mysterious developer launched Bitcoin at the beginning of 2009. Encoded in the first block of transactions was a message highly relevant to the state of global financial affairs at that time:

"The Times 03/Jan/2009 Chancellor on brink of second bailout for banks."

The first block of transactions, called the "Genesis block", set forth Bitcoin, a new peer-to-peer digital currency. As the quoted headline was published by The Times on January 3, 2009, the message acts as proof that the block was indeed created after that time. From the intention of the comment on the failure of fractional reserve lending, we get a glimpse into the mind of its developer, Satoshi Nakamoto.

More importantly, Bitcoin and its technology, the Blockchain, was released and open sourced to the world. The Bitcoin Blockchain was a solution to the difficult problem of preventing double spending when creating a distributed virtual currency.

Double spending occurs when two transactions are accepted with an amount that exceeds the available balance. Up until that time, a decentralized solution to the double spending problem remained open. Satoshi's solution was the Blockchain.

Satoshi Nakamoto

Satoshi Nakamoto has remained anonymous since releasing Bitcoin. Records of his e-mails and forum posts exist from the end of 2008 through 2010. During that time, he worked with developers to release the source code and respond to the development topics. He also commented on relevant financial topics such as banking and fractional reserve lending.

Tip:

Satoshi Nakamoto's e-mails and forum posts have been archived on the website of the Satoshi Nakamoto Institute (http://satoshi.nakamotoinstitute.org). It's a great resource for understanding the intentions behind the design of Bitcoin.

As quickly as he appeared, he vanished without much trace. To this day, we don't have much information on him. Many people have theorized about who Satoshi could be, yet nothing we have is conclusive.

However mysterious his character may be, his legacy remains as the Bitcoin whitepaper.

BITCOIN

The White Paper

The Bitcoin whitepaper was released to the public on October 31st, 2008, a couple of months before Bitcoin's Blockchain was launched. In the whitepaper, Satoshi explained how the Blockchain could support a purely decentralized e-currency without the need for a central authority. Satoshi writes:

"A purely peer-to-peer version of electronic cash would allow online payments to be sent directly from one party to another without the burdens of going through a financial institution."

The whitepaper mentions the issues with relying on the financial institutions as trusted third parties to process transactions. He particularly mentioned the costs of mediating reversible transactions which put merchants at risk of fraud, thus increasing transaction costs. The principal design goal was to ensure that whoever owns the keys controls the money. The common scenario involves a buyer who orders an item from a merchant using a credit card. As fraud against the merchant, the buyer can dispute the payment or claim an unauthorized payment. In Bitcoin, reversing the transaction is not possible.

Satoshi proposed a solution that relies on cryptographic proof. Transactions are signed and distributed on a public network. The design allows irreversible transactions sent directly between peers without centralized authority.

He was able to deliver the solution, based on a new type of data structure called the Blockchain.

The Blockchain

The public ledger which records each Bitcoin transaction is built on a data structure called the Blockchain. Transactions are grouped into blocks, and shared and validated by a network of nodes. Consensus on the network determines which blocks are accepted.

Previously, the double-spending problem was difficult to solve without a trusted third party. To be able to accept a transaction, the available balance had to be validated by a central authority, ensuring synchronization between all the transactions.

Implementing this in a decentralized way was difficult because of the complexities of sharing data between independent nodes. If two transactions were created at the same time, but with only enough funds available for the first transaction, the second must be rejected: the double spending problem.

As we examine the Blockchain, we will see how it solves the double spending problem in a resilient and decentralized way.

Keys, transactions, and blocks

To help you understand how Bitcoin transactions work, we'll need to explain how some of its basic mechanisms work with various cryptographic algorithms. With the classic example of sending money between Alice and Bob, we will illustrate how the Bitcoin network confirms a transaction.

BITCOIN

Creating a transaction

Let's start with an example where Alice wants to send 4.0BTC to Bob. Alice has a Bitcoin wallet with two addresses along with the corresponding private keys that control the two amounts 1.2BTC and 2.8BTC. To receive the money, Bob will generate a private key with a Bitcoin address:

To transfer the Bitcoin, we need to create a valid transaction and broadcast it to the Bitcoin network for confirmation. If confirmed by the network, the transferred amount will be available for spending by the receiver.

The transaction can record a transfer between two or more parties, using many inputs for the sources of Bitcoin and many outputs for the receivers of Bitcoin. Inputs and outputs are used to move the money between the addresses.

Each input must reference exactly one output from a previous transaction. Thus, on the Blockchain, Bitcoin is sent through scripts which hand-off the money between the addresses. As each address is controlled by a private key, the money is transferred between the owners of the private keys. There is sometimes the misconception that there is a single Bitcoin that gets moved, when in fact there is no Bitcoin, or fraction of Bitcoin, that is individually assigned to an address.

Transfers of Bitcoins are actually controlled by matching the inputs and outputs of the previous transactions. Thus, the full history of transactions funding the transaction are needed to validate a transfer.

Before broadcasting the transaction, we'll need to prove to the network that Alice was the original sender of the transaction.

By proving to the network that we have the private keys, the nodes validating the transaction can agree that the transaction originated from the owner.

Digital signatures

One classic problem addressed by cryptography is how one party can send a document to another party with proof that it was not modified or forged. For example, let's say Alice has a message that she wants to send to Bob. Before trusting the document, Bob wants to be sure that the message has not been modified.

Alice needs a way to digitally sign the document with proof that it's an exact copy of the original document. Using a digital signature, Bob can verify the copy. If valid, he can be sure that the document has not been modified.

Digital signatures rely on a set of keys designated as public and private. Signing a document with a private key creates a signature that can be verified with its associated public key. Any signed document verified by the public key can be assumed to be original.

Public key encryption

Public key encryption is a cryptographic algorithm that uses two mathematically generated keys to encrypt and decrypt a message, or to digitally sign a document. The private key is used to encrypt or sign the document, and the public key is used to decrypt the message or verify the signature.

The two keys are generated at the same time by an asymmetric cryptographic algorithm. The keys are mathematically bound and cannot be interchanged. In other words, the public key only functions with its corresponding private key.

Public and private keys are simply long numbers. An example private key looks as follows:

308201130201010420 9ea335d666d9e097c5a5e92ef3 2228a18c3615aa38e13f b593712a11f039c148a081a530 81a2020101302c06072a8648ce3d0101022100ffffffffff ffffffffffffffffffffffffffffffffffffffffeffffffc2f300604010 004010704410479be667ef9dcbbac55a06295ce870b0 7029bfcdb2dce28d959f2815b16f81798483ada7726a3c 4655da4fbfc0e1108a8fd17b448a68554199c47d08ffb1 0d4b802210 0ffffffffffffffffffffffffffffffffebaaedce6af48a 03bbfd25e8cd0364141020101a14403420004a6b634e b85a8d9d6fe34bc666676 0b3343c40f7709392541bc2 d3b7666eda4d7c7c8dd578af2790870a591c0f17e285ce 99cb2dd950b37b00f1031675bb678d6

Its public key looks as shown next:

04a6b634eb85a8d9d6fe34bc666676 0b3343c40f7709 392541bc2d3b7666eda4d7c7c8dd578af2790870a591c 0f17e285ce99cb2dd950b37b00f1031675bb678d6

These two keys are mathematically related and cannot be interchanged with any other key.

Signing a document

In the example with Alice and Bob using encryption software, Alice creates a public and private key pair. She then sends a copy of the public key to Bob. As the public key can only be generated by the private key, Bob can assume that Alice is the holder of the private key.

Before sending the document to Bob, Alice signs the document with her private key and includes the signature in the document.

Later, when Bob receives the document, he can verify the signature with the copy of the document. If the signature is valid, Bob can safely assume that Alice was the signer:

Elliptic Curve Cryptography

Bitcoin uses Elliptic Curve Digital Signature Algorithms (ECDSA), for generating public/private key pairs. The algorithm generates random keys based on the mathematics around elliptic curves.

Due to its features, ECDSA is suitable for signing Bitcoin transactions. For example, some algorithms can only generate both keys at the same time. With the ECDSA algorithm, a public key can be generated from a private key at any time, but not the other way around.

Bitcoin addresses

Bitcoin addresses are generated from the public key through a few steps that involve cryptographic hashes. To explain the process, we'll first introduce cryptographic hashing algorithms.

BITCOIN

Generating a Bitcoin address

Bitcoin addresses are generated from the public key hash of an ECDSA key pair. Let's walk through a simplified explanation of this process with the following pair:

Private Key:

18E14A7B6A307F426A94F8114701E7C8E774E7F9A47E2C2035D-

B29A206321725

Public Key Hash:

600FFE422B4E00731A59557A5CCA46C-

C183944191006324A447BDB2D98D4B408

To generate the Bitcoin address, SHA256 and RIPEMD-160 hashing functions are first applied to the public key:

010966776006953D5567439E5E39F86A0D273BEE

To identify which network the address is intended for, a network identifier is added to the front of the address. In the preceding example, we simply add 00, which identifies the main network, to the beginning of the key:

00010966776006953D5567439E5E39F86A0D273BEE

Next, a checksum is calculated. Checksums are used to ensure that the address has a valid set of characters. That is, if one of the characters is mistyped, the checksum digit will be invalid. Thus, Bitcoin wallets can use the checksum to make sure you

Chapter 2 – Understanding the Blockchain

didn't enter a bogus Bitcoin address. In the previous example, the checksum is calculated as "D61967F6" and appended to the end of the string:

000109667760069530D5567439E5E39F86A0D273BEED61967F6

Finally, a BASE58 function is applied to the network identifier, hash, and checksum. BASE58 is a way to encode large numeric values into an alphanumeric string of characters. The BASE58 value can be easily read or written by humans, making it practical for creating Bitcoin public addresses.

16UwLL9Risc3QfPqBUvKofHmBQ7wMtjvM

The result is a public address we can use to receive Bitcoin and the private key needed to spend them. Using our Bitcoin wallet or other tools, we can generate unlimited random private keys and their addresses. This process is usually automated.

In summary, we create a private key and its Bitcoin address by starting with a large random number. An Elliptic Curve algorithm is used to generate the private/public key pair from the random number. Finally, the Bitcoin address is generated by transforming the public key through several hashing functions, appending a checksum, and encoding it with BASE58.

Signing a transaction

The last step needed before broadcasting the transaction to the network is to include a digital signature.

Using the private keys from each input address listed, the sender can prove that they have ownership of the funds stored in the address. The network can then verify the signature with access to the public key. Transactions with invalid digital signatures are simply discarded.

At any point, the private key is never shared. Once signed, our valid transaction is now ready to broadcast to the Bitcoin network for confirmation.

Decentralized network

The Bitcoin network consists of many thousands of nodes, with some called miners, and each connected directly to one another. Unlike a centralized or distributed network, Bitcoin relies on a decentralized network.

A decentralized network is extremely resilient because there is no central point of failure. If one or more nodes are taken offline, the remaining nodes can reroute their connection to the network through other online nodes.

In fact, the early incarnation of the Internet, called ARPANET and built by the US Department of Defense, used a decentralized design to build an information network that would be able to function even if a large portion of the network was down.

Bitcoin is a money protocol that is built on a decentralized network. Each node is independent and can join or leave the network at any time. While on the network, each node can talk to the other nodes using the Bitcoin protocol. With this

Chapter 2 – Understanding the Blockchain

protocol, it's able to script and validate the transactions or other types of digital contracts.

Bitcoin is essentially programmable money designed to run on a decentralized network.

Broadcasting the transaction

To broadcast our signed transaction to the network, we first need to connect to one or more of the existing nodes. When connected, our node becomes part of the network and is able to send and receive transactions.

The nodes on the network listen for broadcasted transactions and share them with the other nodes. Each node can maintain a copy of every transaction created, and use them to validate new Bitcoin transactions and ensure there's sufficient balance before relaying them to the other nodes.

New transactions broadcasted to the network are initially labeled as unconfirmed, meaning that the network has not yet agreed that they are valid. A transaction must have sufficient balance and a valid digital signature before it can be validated.

Valid transactions are grouped into a block by the miner. After a verification process, which involves a difficult mathematical problem, the confirmed blocks are accepted and exchanged between the nodes. The blocks of transactions are time-stamped and chained together to form a "Blockchain". Each node maintains its own copy of the Blockchain and repeats the process by listening for new transactions.

The Blockchain

Bitcoin uses a unique and novel way of storing and distributing its transaction ledger. To create a database of transactions that is both resilient and transparent, it distributes all its transactions across a global network of nodes. This database is called the Blockchain. To understand how the Blockchain works, we'll explore how the blocks are used to group and distribute the transactions.

Blocks

The Blockchain is a chain of blocks linked together, from the Genesis block to the latest block. Every node connected to the network maintains a complete copy of the entire Blockchain. This redundancy results in a very resilient system.

New blocks are mined by the nodes listening for transactions on the network. The nodes can share and relay the transactions amongst themselves. When a new transaction is received by a node, it is added to the new block. The new block is kept locally until a difficult computing problem is solved using the new block as the base of the solution.

New blocks with solutions to the difficult problem are eligible for a reward of newly mined Bitcoin, plus the transaction fees included with each transaction.

Referring back to cryptographic hashes, a hash value is used to represent the confirmation of the block. A hash value is computed on the block and its transactions, along with the hash value of the previous block. Any changes to the block can be validated against its hash.

Chapter 2 – Understanding the Blockchain

The chains of hashes are critical to the integrity of the chain. Each new block contains within it the hash of the previous block. If any of the transactions are modified, the hash, as well as the rest of the chain, becomes invalid. Therefore, as the chain grows and more copies of it are maintained by independent miners, the more difficult it becomes to modify the public ledger.

Today, the Bitcoin network's combined computing power is noted as the largest supercomputer on earth. The large amount of computer power is what protects the Bitcoin network from attacks. Any attacker would need to overtake more than half of the network's computer power to be able to double spend.

The result is a database of transactions that are distributed for redundancy and cryptographically protected from modifications. Anyone can download a copy of the Blockchain and query it for transactions. With the full Blockchain, the value of any address can be known for any point in time. The addresses with unspent balances can then be used as inputs to a new transaction.

Forks

Due to their independent nature, the network of nodes can consist of either honest or malicious nodes. Honest nodes only accept valid transactions and reject any that double spend or have invalid signatures. Malicious nodes may make an attempt to accept a corrupt transaction or selectively reject the other transactions.

BITCOIN

To isolate and reject the bad nodes on the network, consensus between the nodes exists on what rule set to accept. This consensus determines which blocks are accepted on the network. Since the Genesis block, a large majority of the nodes have agreed to "play nicely" rather than to corrupt, due to the reward of earning new Bitcoin. This consensus forms the longest and most trustworthy chain.

Due to changes in how the nodes can accept/reject blocks, it is possible for the Blockchain to fork and create a side Blockchain.

If a corrupted block is detected by the network, the result is a fork in the chain. Without validations from the network, the blocks become orphans and the fork invalid. Valid blocks are added to the valid portion of the chain. From the network's perspective, the longest chain of valid blocks is considered the official Blockchain. From any block, there is one path back to the Genesis block.

Blocks from shorter chains are called orphans. Orphans are eventually abandoned and not used for anything. All the valid transactions included in the shorter chain are copied and added to a new block, and eventually integrated into the longer chain.

Bug fixes or major version updates can also cause a fork in the Blockchain. As new nodes implement a version update, the result can be a fork and change. This is how the Bitcoin network accepts or rejects the changes to the protocol and software.

Chapter 2 – Understanding the Blockchain

Therefore, it's possible to have multiple versions of the software evolve through the Blockchain.

In summary, all the nodes connected to the Bitcoin network can relay transactions. The nodes are connected to each other through a decentralized network. To validate transactions, each node maintains a full copy of the Blockchain. The Blockchain is built from a chain of blocks. Each block contains a list of valid transactions and is linked to the previous block in the chain.

While all the nodes help to build the Bitcoin network, some nodes can choose to mine for new Bitcoins. These nodes are called miners. Mining is the process of using a new block of transactions as the base to a difficult puzzle to solve with computational power. If it is solved, the miner is rewarded new Bitcoins, plus the transaction fees included with each transaction.

The Bitcoin supply

The total number of Bitcoins is fixed at 21 million and is distributed as a reward to the miners who solve a difficult computing problem. Rewards are given out approximately every 10 minutes, depending on the total number of miners competing for the reward. The difficulty of the problem is adjusted, to compensate for the changes in the number of miners competing, every two weeks.

Starting with the Genesis block in the year 2009, 50 Bitcoins were released as rewards. After every 210,000 blocks, the reward is halved to compensate for the anticipated increase in global computer power. It takes about four years to mine 210,000 blocks.

To earn the mining reward, a miner must broadcast proof, called proof of work, that they have solved a difficult computing problem.

Proof of work

Miners compete for the Bitcoin reward by submitting a "proof of work" to the network. Generating the proof of work involves the computation of a hash value on the block. The miner is looking for the smallest hash value possible.

The target value, called difficulty, is published by the network. If the hash value of the new block is less than the difficulty value published, then the miner has found a valid solution that is eligible as proof of work.

Blocks are accepted on the network as other miners confirm the proof of work.

Confirmation

If another miner accepts the proof of work, the miner is awarded the new Bitcoins and that block becomes the next block in the longest Blockchain. All transactions grouped in the block are given a confirmation. All miners then start the process of mining on top of that chain.

As more blocks are added to the chain, the confirmation count for each transaction is increased. The more confirmations the transaction has, the more difficult it is to modify the chain of blocks.

Difficulty level

As competition for the Bitcoin reward can vary based on the number of miners on the network, the difficulty level can be adjusted to keep the reward rate at approximately once every 10 minutes.

The difficulty level is calculated from the rate at which the last blocks were accepted. If the rate of blocks found is less than 10 minutes, the difficulty will be increased; if it takes more than 10 minutes, it's decreased. The difficulty level is updated every 2,016 blocks.

Mining

When a node is actively searching for a hash value below the difficulty level, it is considered a miner. The actual process of mining includes listening for transactions to create the new block which is used to compute the hash value. Collectively, all the nodes on the network follow a basic workflow for mining:

- New transactions are broadcasted to the network. The nodes relay new transactions to the other nodes. New transactions are initially marked as unconfirmed.

- Each node collects and validates the transactions into a new block. The nodes continuously listen for new transactions and update the block as needed.

- Each node looks for the solution to a difficult problem that involves computing a hash of the block. The solution to the problem includes finding a hash value that's less than the published target.

- If a solution is found, it's broadcasted to the network. The solution consists of the block of transactions and the hash value. The proof is easily verified by the other nodes on the network.

- If all the transactions in the block and its hash value are valid, the block becomes the longest chain. All miners begin mining on top of that chain and the process is repeated.

Solving a difficult problem

The goal of every miner is to produce a block of transactions with a hash value that's lower than the difficulty level published by the network. It would be extremely unlikely that computing the very first hash of a block of transaction will produce this hash value.

To allow another try, the Bitcoin protocol allows the miners to add a nonce to the end of the transaction, which is ignored by the network.

The nonce is a simple number that is incremented for each try. Each increment of the nonce results in another unique hash value. Since the hash values can be radically different from just a single character change, a large range of values is generated.

Mining is highly competitive. In the beginning, it was common for a laptop computer to solve the puzzle. Today, however, it requires special hardware that can perform billions or even trillions of hashes per second.

Included in the new block is a Bitcoin address created by the miner. Once a valid hash value is found, the block is broadcasted to the network. If accepted, the new block becomes part of the chain and the new Bitcoin reward is officially minted. Coins are generally accepted, after 100 blocks, as money that is available to spend.

Transaction fees

Transaction fees are small amounts paid to the miner for confirming your transaction. In some cases a fee is not required, but by paying a fee you are contributing to the incentive to mine.

The fee requirements are based on a ruleset accepted by the network. One rule is used to prevent payments intended to spam the network. If your transaction is less than 0.01BTC then a transaction fee of 0.0001BTC is required.

A transaction fee can be required, based on the miner, if the transaction size exceeds 10,000 bytes. A transaction can include many inputs and outputs which are simply stored as bytes in a record. The total number of bytes is the total transaction size. A simple way to estimate the size of a transaction is by using the following formula:

Size in bytes = 148 * number of inputs + 34 * number of outputs + 10

Lastly, transaction fees are used to prioritize old and high-value coins. Based on the inputs listed in your transaction, a function is used to calculate the average age by the size of the transaction. If it is below a specific threshold, then a fee will be required. To simplify the priority calculations, one can assume that a single bitcoin can be spent one day after receiving it without paying a fee.

Fees are deducted directly from the transaction, reducing the output total by the amount of the fee. There is no output allocated specifically for the transaction fee.

Rules for requiring a transaction fee are shared similarly between the miners. However, each miner has the option of choosing which rules to implement. It is possible for a miner to accept any valid transaction without a fee. However, the majority that require a fee can delay or ignore transactions that bypass the fee structure.

Therefore, to improve the chance of having your transaction confirmed as quickly as possible, it's best to follow the documented transaction fee structure.

Network attacks

The Bitcoin network is protected by the consensus of the network. Valid transactions and changes to the software must be accepted by the majority of the miners on the network. Let's discuss the attacks that could occur:

51 percent attacks

It is theoretically possible for a large amount of computing power to overtake the network and accept double spending or prevent confirmations. This is called the 51 percent attack.

Although theoretically possible, the opposing argument to the attack notes the amount of computing power needed to perform the attack. Some argue that it is not financially feasible to execute the attack as the network could quickly reject the malicious blocks. It would be difficult for a large pool of nodes to produce a segment of the Blockchain of more than six blocks in a row with a corrupt transaction.

Race attacks

A malicious spender could try to double spend by broadcasting two transactions to the network at the same time. Given that the merchant would accept a transaction without any confirmation, it's possible to double spend in this way.

The quick antidote to this attack is to simply wait for confirmation of both the transactions.

Finney attacks

The Finney attack is named after the Bitcoin developer Hal Finney. In this attack, a miner must pre-mine one transaction into a new block and spend the coins before releasing the block. If the payment is still unconfirmed, the new block will include a double spending transaction. The solution is to wait for at least six confirmations.

Alternative coins

The Bitcoin software is open source and available to the public. From the public repository, many "alternative coins" have been created by copying the source code and re-configuring specific parameters. Each alt-coin can implement a different ruleset independent of any other alt-coin.

BITCOIN

Generally, alt-coins implement different quantities for the total money supply or different block rates. For example, Litecoin has a total supply of 84 million coins and a mining rate of approximately two minutes.

Other alt-coins may implement a built-in inflation. For example, Freicoin has a built-in demurrage that's 5 percent per year. Basically, if you hold 1 Freicoin, it will be worth 5 percent less if you spend it one year later. This was used as an incentive to promote spending.

As another interesting coin, Namecoin uses its Blockchain to record information about the ownership of names. The most popular use for this mechanism is to record the ownership of domain names. Using the Namecoin Blockchain, one can earn Namecoins by mining and using the coins to purchase one's own .bit domain name.

The world of alt-coins is changing rapidly, with many new ideas being tested. Yet, it is not uncommon to see the rise and fall of new alt-coins. One should investigate the size and history of any alt-coin before investing.

Chapter 3:

The Mining Process

The Bitcoin network distributes newly-minted Bitcoin through a novel approach called mining. By voluntarily supplying raw computing power, miners serve the network by validating and confirming Bitcoin transactions. In return, the miners are awarded Bitcoins from a limited supply. Along with each award, they collect fees included with the transactions they choose to validate.

Bitcoin mining, an important aspect of the network, is highly competitive and involves many technical factors. In this chapter, we will explore the mining process in more detail. With this base understanding of the process, we will be able to understand the feasibility of mining.

In this chapter, we will discuss the following topics:

- Explanation of the mining ecosystem, mining pools, and available hardware
- Setting up a mining client
- Connecting to a mining pool

- Introduction to tools to help calculate the feasibility of mining

Digital gold

The first humans certainly had an advantage with regards to finding precious materials such as gold and silver. It's easy to imagine flakes or small nuggets of gold naturally exposed by streams and lakes. Human beings walking around the area could easily collect them for trade or utility.

As time went on, more and more of the easily available precious metals and gems were picked. Miners continued their search deeper and deeper into the earth, risking their lives and wealth in search for these valuable materials.

With the expansion of human civilization to new lands and continents, new sources were found. In 1849, gold was found in a stream near Coloma, California. After the news broke, hundreds of thousands of miners, called the 49ers, rushed out to California in search of the gold.

Within a few years, most of the easily found gold was picked, driving the miners to use more advanced techniques. By the mid-1850s, the miners had adopted hydraulic mining equipment and other mechanical means to extract the gold. It was a difficult process and successful mining required skill and luck.

Bitcoin mining

The 1849 California Gold Rush is analogous to the beginning of Bitcoin's mining story. They both share similar characteristics.

First, both gold and Bitcoin have a limited supply. The amount of gold on the planet is fixed and cannot increase. Similarly, Bitcoin's algorithm is designed to ensure that only a fixed amount of Bitcoin will be found.

In both cases, the early miners had better results mining in the beginning. In the case of the 49ers, within the first 2 years much of the gold found was easily picked from streams and rivers. With Bitcoin mining, the number of Bitcoins awarded to the miners decreases over time. The new reward block halves every 4 years and the mining difficulty increases, as its adjusted every two weeks based on the competition to mine. Thus, many early adopters were able to easily mine more than 50 Bitcoins a day using a standard computer with a fast processor or a graphics processor.

Today, mining for gold is an expensive operation and is generally left to large mining companies funded by large investments of capital. The same holds true for Bitcoin. Large mining companies and pools exist, driving the competition to find Bitcoin way up.

The golden years of Bitcoin mining may be behind us, but the process of mining still plays an important role in the Bitcoin ecosystem. In addition to earning newly minted Bitcoins, the miners also earn transaction fees. These fees are paid by the sender of a Bitcoin transaction and create an incentive for the miners to quickly confirm their transaction.

Having a large base of miners is important to Bitcoin as it builds trust in the network. The larger the base of miners, the more difficult it is to overtake the network.

As we've seen with many of the alt-coins that have been released, without any significant base of miners, there's very little trust in the currency. Ultimately, it yields a low exchange rate with little demand for the currency.

Let's begin by exploring the various aspects involved with mining a Bitcoin.

Exploring the mining ecosystem

Bitcoin mining provides the network with two very important processes: the creation of new Bitcoin and the confirmation of transactions.

As discussed in **Chapter 2, Understanding the Blockchain**, the miners listen for new and valid transactions to combine them into a new block. The block represents a scope around a group of transactions that can be easily validated against the previous blocks. Structuring the ledger this way makes the processing of transactions easy to distribute.

From the perspective of the miner, a new block is potentially valuable. The bytes from the block are used as the base for computing an answer to a difficult computing problem. The miners make many millions of attempts at solving the

Chapter 3 – The Mining Process

difficult computing problem in hope of finding the solution before any other miner.

If found, the miner quickly broadcasts the solution to the network to make the claim. If it is confirmed by the network, the miner receives the new Bitcoin, as well as all the fees included with each transaction in the block. The new block then serves as the latest block in the Blockchain. The miners then start the race again by listening for new transactions and repeating the process.

Validating transactions

Each transaction broadcasted to the network must be checked for double spending, that is, sending more Bitcoin than what's available, and for a valid digital signature. To confirm the available balance, the miner must have a validated copy of the entire Blockchain.

After installing a Bitcoin node, a client will connect to the network and begin requesting each block sequentially from the other nodes on the network. After checking each block against the previous blocks, one by one, the Blockchain is replicated and stored locally.

The local copy of the Blockchain contains every transaction from the beginning of time. This ledger is maintained and used to validate the spending balance of each new transaction. If a transaction is found to be invalid, it is simply ignored and discarded.

The second check requires validation of the digital signature. Using cryptographic algorithms, the miner is able to check the signature attached to the transaction to validate the integrity of the transaction. Any modification to the transaction will result in an invalid signature, and thus the miner is able to confirm that the transaction to be processed was the original version sent from the holder of the private key.

With a list of valid transactions, the miner assembles a new block and uses it as the base for solving a difficult computing problem.

Proof-of-Work

In **Chapter 2, Understanding the Blockchain** we described a hash as the result of a mathematical function applied to a set of data. In our case, the data is the new block of valid transactions. When a hashing function is applied to the data, a numerical value is returned. If we change any byte of the data and re-compute the hash, we'll get a completely new hash value that's radically different to the original.

Mining involves using the hash function to generate a hash result. If the hash result matches the target, it's considered the solution. If the result is invalid, throwaway number called a nonce is added to the data. The data set is then hashed again, giving the miner another try. This process is repeated until a solution is found.

When a solution is found, it's broadcast to the network as a new block, which also contains the difficulty target and the winning nonce. This is called proof-of-work. The other nodes on the network can re-compute the hash on the block and the nonce to verify the proof-of-work.

If accepted, the new block becomes part of the Blockchain. The nodes that agree on the solution then share the new block with

Chapter 3 – The Mining Process

the other nodes on the network. The end result is that the new Bitcoins and the transaction fees collected are awarded to the winning miner.

SHA-256

Computing a hash value is computationally expensive. To produce the proof-of-work, the hashing function is executed many times until a valid hash is found. Thus, the work is described as "solving a difficult computing problem".

Bitcoin uses a hash function called **SHA-256**. It's a secure cryptographic hash function that can be computed by software, or more efficiently by hardware.

Specifically, the miners are looking for a hash value that's less than the target value. They will perform many millions of hashes per second looking for the winning hash result. Since any small change to the data set produces a different hash value, a nonce is added to the set. Each retry of the hash includes an increment to the nonce. When incremented, the resulting hash is completely different to the previous hash. This gives the miner another chance at finding a hash value that's lower than the published difficulty level.

Scrypt

Litecoin, as well as many other alt-coins, uses a different configuration for the hashing algorithm. Scrypt also uses SHA-256 for hashing, but with an additional algorithm called Salsa20, which requires a large amount of memory, or RAM, to compute. Thus, the scrypt algorithm is not only computationally expensive; it's memory intensive as well.

The rationale behind using an additional component, in this case, a large amount of RAM, is to make it harder to scale the mining process using computer processors alone. This gives those with access to individual computers an advantage over the mining operations that scale with processors.

Mining rewards

Newly minted Bitcoins are awarded for proof-of-work confirmed by the network. The number of Bitcoins awarded is set on a curve, which halves every 210,000 blocks.

The first rewards were set at 50 bitcoins. After approximately four years, the first 210,000 blocks were mined and the reward was reduced by half to 25. The rate will continue halving, to 12.5, 6.25, and so on, until the last fraction of a bitcoin is found. The total number of bitcoins is fixed at 21,000,000 and the smallest fraction is 0.00000001.

Note:

The smallest unit of Bitcoin is called a Satoshi, named after its developer.

The curve, which declines in half over time, is intended to offset the anticipated increase in available computing power. In other words, as the cost of computing power decreases, the difficulty of earning the reward increases to balance the equation.

As competition for the rewards increases, the rate of solutions found to the difficult computing problem will increase. With more miners searching for the solution, the average rate could

Chapter 3 – The Mining Process

become less than the intended rate of one new block every 10 minutes.

To offset this, a difficulty level is calculated and adjusted every 2016 blocks. The calculation considers the last two weeks of transactions to produce a target difficulty. If the average is below the 10 minute average, the difficulty is increased, and if it is above, the difficulty is decreased. Using the difficulty metrics, a miner can make some basic predictions about how much computing power will be required to mine a single Bitcoin.

Mining hardware

In Bitcoin's early days, standard CPUs were used to compute the hashes. Included in the original Bitcoin client was a feature that allowed you to use the CPU to mine. In the early days of Bitcoin, it was easy for a single CPU to earn a full award of Bitcoin. However, as the number of miners increased, CPUs quickly became obsolete for mining.

As mining competition increased, software was adapted to utilize graphic processing units (GPUs). GPUs are optimized to perform mathematical operations many times faster than CPUs. They are used to accelerate the computation of complex graphics applications, such as computer gaming and rendering. Because of their optimizations, they are well suited to performing the mathematical operations needed to quickly compute a hash.

The mining operators often maintain racks of GPUs. Several graphics cards could be connected to one computer. This resulted in the generation of large amounts of heat. To

55

maintain peak performance of the equipment, air conditioning units were required to keep it cool.

Soon after the GPUs were adopted as the standard for mining, computer chip manufacturers began developing microchips that performed the hashing computations directly. This resulted in a large increase in the number of hash performed per second, with a fraction of the electricity needed.

Initially, Field-Programmable Gate Arrays, (FPGAs) were configured and used for building the mining rigs. These are special integrated chips that allow a programmer to encode the hardware level instruction to be executed directly on the chip. They provided the miners with fast hashing speeds and used much less electricity.

Application Specific Integrated Chips (ASICs) quickly became the hot item for mining. These chips could perform billions of hashes per second while using far less power.

In Bitcoin mining, all the CPU and GPU, and most FPGA, processors have been replaced by the ASIC mining hardware. Due to the competition and the costs involved, mining with anything other than an ASIC is not viable.

Mining conditions

Due to the demands placed on the equipment, it's crucial that it be kept and maintained in a proper environment to sustain conditions for peak performance.

Most notable are the cooling requirements. Air conditioning may be required to maintain a constant temperature for the

Chapter 3 – The Mining Process

equipment to operate. Make sure that you factor a cooling system into your budget and design.

Electricity usage from both the equipment and the cooling must be assessed and arranged. Clean and stable electricity is important so as to not damage the equipment. Electrical spikes and high loads can cause interruptions to your mining operation.

Constant monitoring of the equipment is important. Downtime could result in a much lower return on investment than anticipated. Thus, it is common for serious mining operations to have a full time staff to monitor the conditions and maintain the equipment.

Mining pools

It can be quite difficult for a single ASIC miner to find the necessary proof-of-work to earn the rewards from a new block. This is especially true if every miner on the network is working individually as well. Thus, the chances of earning the Bitcoin are either all or nothing with regards to a single block reward. To improve the chances of earning the Bitcoin, a strategy for mining called pooling exists.

The mining operators are able to join together their collective power to form mining pools. As a group, their chances of finding the difficult to generate proof-of-work become much better. Upon winning the reward, the pool agrees to share the profits based on the work contributed by the individual miners.

Mining pools give lower powered miners an advantage because it can be very difficult for them to earn a full block alone. When operating as part of a collective, their computing power is awarded based on the amount of computing power provided.

Mining shares

In a pool, the work is measured in shares. One share is issued for each proof-of-work submitted. However, in the case of a mining pool, the proof-of-work is accepted based on the easiest difficulty level.

At the easiest difficulty level, a much larger range of nonces are eligible as the solution to the computing problem. Proof-of-work generated against an easy difficulty level is how the individual miners are able to prove to the pool that they have been working.

Eventually, when a share meets the network's difficulty level, the whole pool earns the reward, as it is divided and distributed to the individual miners based on the shares submitted.

Fees and Payout

The mining pools charge fees, typically ranging from 0.5 percent to 3.0 percent, depending on the payout method. Based on the payout methods, the mining pool operator may be at risk from a miner who cheats about the share reported. Generally, the more risk the mining operates assumes, the higher the fees.

A round is usually used in the calculation and represents the current block being mined. After a new block has been found, the round is closed and another is started.

Payout from the mining operator is based on various methods. Some methods are optimized for quicker payouts, while others give incentives for new shares. The various methods are designed to reduce or prevent cheating. The mining pools use different methods, along with competitive fees, to encourage miners to join their pool.

Cloud mining

Mining contracts are available for those who wish to outsource the mining process to another company. Companies offering Cloud Mining services allow one to purchase a contract for a specific amount of time and hash rate. The service operates similarly to the mining pool process.

The advantages of cloud mining are obvious, as the buyer doesn't have to own the equipment, maintain it, and manage its uptime. All the equipment is based in a remote data center and is maintained by the cloud mining company.

However, the buyer must beware. The returns on profit can be much lower than a normal investment. Furthermore, there have been scams reported and losses from malicious companies. Make sure that you do your research on a service before paying for any services or contracts.

Estimating profitability

There are many factors involved in estimating mining profitability. The significant variables are hardware costs, electricity, and mining difficulty.

Hardware efficiency

Starting with the hardware, one must consider the hashing speed of the equipment against the power used. A simple formula for evaluating the mining efficiency would consider these two variables:

Hashes per second / power consumption = efficiency

Hardware efficiency calculations are useful for evaluating the hardware. Be aware that the hash rates published by the vendors could vary from the actual rates. Additionally, it may take some time for the equipment to arrive. Make sure that you do some research on the forums to see what hash rates the other customers are getting.

Factoring in the difficulty level

One must compare the difficulty rate against the available hardware to project an estimate of the possible returns. Using some simple math, the rewards from mining at a specified hash rate can be estimated.

We start with the hash rate:

Hashes = number of hashes per second

Given that there are 86,400 seconds in a day, we can calculate the number of hashes per day:

Hashes * 86400 = hashes per day

The chance of a hash being a valid share is approximately one in 2^{32}:

Chapter 3 – The Mining Process

(Hashes * 86400) / 2^32 = shares per day

Factoring in the difficulty level, we can estimate that the shares' chances of being the solution to a new block is as follows:

(Hashes * 86400) / (2^32 difficulty) = blocks per day

Finally, we apply the block reward:

(Hashes * 86400 * reward) / (2^32 * difficulty) = average Bitcoins per day

Using the formula, we can make a quick estimate of the average number of Bitcoins we can earn per day, based on some published hardware statistics.

For example, given today's difficulty level, 49,692,386,355, and a block reward of 25BTC, we can estimate the return of a high performance ASIC miner.

Using the Spondoolies SP35 Yukon for our example, its listed performance is 5.5tera-hashes. Thus, the average daily return would be as follows:

(5500000000000 * 86400 * 25) / (2^32 * 49692386355) = 0.05566301499 BTC

This is only an estimated Bitcoin return, based on the difficulty and the hashing rate. For a more elaborate estimate of mining profitability, one would also include the hardware costs, the electricity rates, and the maintenance costs.

Selecting a currency

When looking to estimate profitability, it's important to consider the crypto-currency with the best chances of making a profit. Difficulty level and exchange rate are the two important variables involved.

With over 500 alt-coins in existence, a miner has a large set of options to choose from. To help with analyzing the data, one can rely on some tools to help with the calculations.

Coinwarz (www.coinwarz.com) is a useful site for evaluating profitability across the various crypto-coins.

Coinwarz maintains difficulty statistics, exchange rates, and volumes, and uses them to give a historical view of profit rations. Using this information, one can make an educated guess about the various trends happening between crypto currencies and optimize their chances for an investment in mining.

Exchange rates

The current exchange rate for the currency you are mining is an unpredictable factor in calculating mining profitability. Many miners have an optimistic view of Bitcoin for the long term, yet in the short term, the volatility leads to uncertainty with mining investments.

Given the risks, we can still make some broad assumptions and use calculators to give us a range of returns.

Chapter 3 – The Mining Process

The Coinwarz website offers some useful tools for calculating future earnings based on hash rates, difficulty, electricity costs, and block rewards.

Setting up a mining client

After doing the proper analysis of costs and return on investment, one may decide if it's the right time to proceed with setting up a mining operation.

Requirements

In general, you'll need to have the proper conditions to set up a basic mining operation. To start with, we'll briefly cover the essentials: capital, hardware, facilities, and availability.

Capital

Most return on investment calculations for Bitcoin mining show profitability over a period of time exceeding one year. The assumption made for the projection includes a stable exchange rate and difficulty level. However, these two factors often vary, which can seriously affect the actual profits.

Essential to starting a mining operation is sufficient capital to carry the operation forward. Before starting the venture, make sure you have enough capital to cover the costs for at least 1 to 2 years, based on the various projected conditions.

Hardware

The purchase of hardware is one of the more volatile aspects of mining. Hardware vendors are constantly designing and improving their equipment. Often, new equipment is pre-sold with several months of backorder time.

Without high-performance hardware, one cannot begin mining. Thus, be sure you have access to a decent set of equipment before securing the rest of your mining operation.

Another aspect to consider when purchasing equipment is the future value of the equipment based on its performance and operational life. Bitcoin mining equipment is changing rapidly and can be outdated within a year. After its useful life is finished, you may have to resell the equipment or recycle it in order to upgrade to new and more powerful equipment.

This was the unfortunate result of a large surge in miners buying the GPU cards. Large orders of GPUs were purchased and used to mine, but when the ASIC chips arrived, the GPUs were quickly replaced. Many miners ended up with large quantities of hardware unusable for mining Bitcoin. Much of the equipment was used for mining other alt-coins or was sold.

Facilities

Early mining enthusiasts started their mining operations from their homes, often in spare bedrooms, garages, or basements. These operations quickly grew into racks and racks of equipment, with fans constantly running as makeshift cooling systems.

The sustainability of these operations running from a personal residence or a family dwelling quickly diminishes. Therefore, it's important to secure a permanent place to set up your mining racks with proper ventilation and cooling.

Chapter 3 – The Mining Process

Easy access to the hardware is important. The ability to diagnose and replace the equipment helps to ensure maximum uptime of your mining operation. Also, one should consider the future expansion of their mining operation. Be sure to plan ahead with space if you plan to grow your operation.

Your mining facilities should include a stable and clean power supply. The mining equipment will pull a constant wattage. Thus, it's important to ensure proper power lines, connections, and outlets to provide adequate wattage.

With all the equipment running at full speed, the sound volume and vibrations can be an issue. Make sure to consider planning for sound proofing the facility if excessive noise is an issue for the neighbors.

Finally, make sure that your facilities are properly protected from theft and other environmental factors, such as flooding and/or earthquakes. It may be possible to have the facilities and its equipment insured. Be sure to check with your agent.

While mining hardware can operate continuously without interruption, a quick response from its operators is important to manage uptime. Hardware and software failures can happen at any time. Without a quick response, the downtime can seriously affect the profitability.

Therefore, it's important to be able to monitor your operations with a quick response time. It is advisable to have a partner or a small team on staff to provide backup or to cover shifts

Choosing the equipment

Procuring high-performance equipment is crucial to the success of your mining operation. As an important aspect of your business, you should research the latest vendors and their equipment.

ASIC miners start in price at around $2,000 and can easily pass $8,000. In addition to the cost of the hardware, you should factor in the equipment's mining efficiency. As mentioned earlier in the chapter, divide the hash rate by the wattage to estimate the equipment's efficiency.

Another metric often used in evaluating equipment's efficiency is Mhash/J or millions of hashes per joule. One joule of energy is equal to one watt of power used for one second. Hashes per joule can be used to evaluate the efficiency over time.

Make sure to factor in the crypto-currencies you're most interested in mining. Many alt-coins use Scrypt and cannot be mined by most ASIC hardware. You'll have to do some research depending on the currency, its difficulty level, and the hardware available to mine it.

Choosing the software

Once you have your hardware purchased and set up with a computer, you'll need to set up the mining software.

The mining software will manage connecting to a mining pool and interacting with the hardware. Part of the process is assigning work from the mining pool to your mining equipment and reporting the shares back to the pool. The two most popular packages are cgminer and BFGMiner.

Cgminer supports ASIC and FPGA Bitcoin mining, and is available for Windows, OS/X, and Linux. It supports connecting with multiple mining pools. You can download the source code from GitHub (https://github.com/ckolivas/cgminer).

Provided with the source code are instructions on how to set up and install the software. Also provided are examples of how to connect to the hardware and the mining pools.

BFGMiner also supports ASIC and FPGA Bitcoin mining and is available for Windows and Linux. It can be downloaded from its website at http://bfgminer.org

With your hardware and software set and ready to work, the next step would be to connect to a mining pool.

Connecting to a mining pool

There are many options available for joining a mining pool, depending on your preferences. You should make an educated decision on which mining pool to use, based on the payout method, the fees charged, and how often a block reward is found. Other features that are nice to have include statistics, easy withdrawal of funds, and various types of merged mining.

The payout method

The payout method can vary between the mining pools. Check the method and the fees included to make sure they match your risk and ability to wait for payouts. Depending on your mining operation's availability, the type of payout may affect your rewards. For example, the miners who do not run stable mining operation will be punished using a score based payout. This means that if your miner gets disconnected for some time, your score may drop to zero.

Also, consider the terms for the payout. Some mining pools release earnings automatically, while others may impose a threshold.

The pool fees

Some pools may charge a fee. The amount usually depends on their assessment of risk and the features they offer. Generally, paying no fees is best, but in some cases, paying a fee could mean better chances of earning a block reward. For example, Deepbit charges 3 percent fees but pays for every solved block, even if it becomes invalid.

The pool speed

The number of rewards earned by a pool is directly related to the overall pool speed. The faster the hash rate for the pool, the more blocks found. In the long term, the rate of rewards found will average out, but with smaller pools you could wait days or weeks to receive a payout.

Additional features

After identifying the payout method, the fees, and the speed that best suits your needs, you can evaluate the pool's additional feature set. Some pools offer nice graphs and statistics, or e-mail notifications and alerts.

Avoiding large pools

The larger the pool size, the more concern there is for it to approach the theoretical 51% attack size. Although there is some debate about how effective the attack would be, the large pools can quickly raise concern in the community.

Generally, miners have more incentive to not join a large pool as it diminishes the overall value of the network. Since the miners are working to earn Bitcoin, they have an interest in keeping the network functioning properly.

There was a case, early in 2014, in which the mining pool GHash.io reached 42% of the network. As the pool size was approaching 51 percent, many miners began voicing the issue and the need to reduce the pool size. Within 24 hours, many miners had left the pool, bringing the size back down to 38 percent.

Running the client

Once your account is setup with the mining pool of choice, you can quickly configure your mining software to connect to the pool and start the mining process.

Assuming you've installed cgminer, simply execute:

cgminer -o http://pool:port -u username -p password

The software will start by connecting to the pool. If everything checks out, the mining software will begin issuing work to your mining equipment

Chapters 4:

Is it Worth Investing in Bitcoins

Although many people have been dismissing Bitcoin as nothing more than just "the magic internet money," this digital currency has continued to soar in value over the few years it has been existence. While many are pointing that this cryptocurrency will offer a very strong competition for the likes of Visa, Western Union, and Paypal, this type of statement misses the point.

Although it's true that Bitcoin protocol could be used as a replacement of these companies at almost no cost, Bitcoin, as the currency, is going head-to-head with fiat money and gold. Bitcoin serves both as a payment system and as a currency, and only a few people would dare say that there's been a better and more efficient payment system ever launched.

The only big and real question left unanswered is whether or not this form of digital currency will have the ability to take a share of the world currency market. When you compare the international currency market with any other industry, you'll notice that there are some great and serious advantages to the Bitcoin over its main competitors.

BITCOIN

Advantages of Bitcoin

Payment freedom: Bitcoin allows you to instantly send and receive money from wherever you are in the world and at any time. No imposed limits. No boundaries.

No bank holidays: This digital currency allows you to be in full control of your money.

Very low fees: Today, Bitcoin payments are processed with extremely small fees or no fees at all. As a Bitcoin user, you can choose to pay a very small fee to receive priority processing; this means faster confirmation of transactions by the Bitcoin network. Besides, the network has merchant processors to help merchants in processing their transactions, converting cryptocurrency to fiat currency and depositing cash directly into the bank accounts of the merchants on a daily basis. Since these services are Bitcoin-based, they are usually offered at a much lower fee than credit card or PayPal networks.

Fewer risks for merchants: All Bitcoin transactions are usually irreversible, secure, and don't contain customer's personal or sensitive information. These features protect merchants from fraudulent losses or fraudulent chargebacks. With Bitcoin, there's no need for PCI compliance. This makes it easy for merchants to expand to new markets where either fraud rates are unacceptably high, or credit cards are not available. The net results are fewer administrative costs, larger markets, and lower transaction fees.

Security and Control: As a Bitcoin user, you will be in full control of your own transactions; merchants can force the unnoticed or unwanted charges just as with any other payment method. You can conduct Bitcoin transactions without providing any personal information. This feature provides strong protection against the common online problem; identity theft. As a Bitcoin user, you can also protect your money with encryption and backup.

Transparent and Neutral: The important information related to the Bitcoin money supply can always be found on the Blockchain for Bitcoin users to verify and use in real-time. Since the Bitcoin protocol is cryptographically secure, no person or organization can manipulate or control it. This enables the Bitcoin's core to be highly trusted for being transparent, neutral, and predictable.

Disadvantages of Bitcoin

Bitcoin still has a few issues that should be worked out, though it's working with some great advantages over its main rivals. Here are the four main problems that should be sorted out to make Bitcoin a good digital currency:

Volatility: The total value of Bitcoins being circulated and the number of businesses and individuals using Bitcoins are very smaller than what they should be. Thus, relatively small business activities, trades, and events can significantly affect the price of this digital currency. Theoretically, the volatility will reduce as Bitcoin markets, as well as the technology, matures. The world has never before seen a start-up digital currency; therefore, it's really hard, and exciting at the same time, to imagine how it will play out.

The degree of acceptance: Today, many people still don't know what Bitcoin is all about. Although more businesses and individuals accept Bitcoins each day simply because they want the advantages of doing so, the list still remains very small and needs to grow for users to benefit from the network effects.

Ongoing development: The software of Bitcoin is still in beta with many of its features still in active development. New services, features, and tools are still being developed to make this cryptocurrency more accessible and secure for the masses.

Some of the features and tools are still not ready for all the users. The majority of Bitcoin businesses are still new and provide no insurance. Bitcoin is still undergoing developments, and it's in the process of maturity.

Not everyone can use Bitcoin: Bitcoin can only be used by people who are good at technology. For instance, your grandma currently will most likely not be able to use Bitcoin. However, this is a temporary issue that can be worked out to be it user-friendly to everybody. Remember, there was a time when seniors found it hard to use credit cards or even email.

With more advancement, Bitcoin will probably become more user-friendly. Today, we are at the "What is the Internet?" stage of Bitcoin. Whether or not people will start walking into McDonald's or Wal-Mart in the near future and pay for items purchased with Bitcoins is an issue that's still up for debate, and no one can deny the fact that this upcoming technology is yet to change the way many people think about money.

There is a possibility of Bitcoins being valueless in the next few years, but it's not possible to imagine a situation where some form of digital currency doesn't challenge the power of the government over the creation of money. In case the government finds out that it cannot win, maybe and just maybe, it will join in on the fun. Of course, this goes against the reason these digital currencies were created in the first place.

Conclusion

The future of finance

Looking back in history, technology has changed the world in profound ways. From the steam engine, to computers, to the Internet, we have seen amazing advances in how we can innovate through technology. In line with the previous advances of technology, Bitcoin has the potential to bring the same scale of change to finance.

Since its launch, just months after the financial crises of 2008, Bitcoin has challenged the way we look at money and finance. Consequently, our previous notions of relying on centralized institutions to issue, store, and transfer money are now questionable.

On the basis of what we've seen from the implementation of new technologies since the industrial revolution, many of our financial institutions face major disruption. The Blockchain's distributed ledger has demonstrated its ability to replace many of the functions they currently service. Yet, to our benefit, as Blockchain's adoption increases, we can expect to see more transparency and credibility on a global scale.

We started the book with a gentle introduction to Bitcoin and how to purchase them within 15 minutes. Helping to understand the basics raises awareness of the responsibility that will be assumed when working with crypto-currencies.

Throughout the book, we explained the mechanism behind the functionality of the Blockchain. As a fundamentally new technology, the algorithms that govern the protocol bring together economic, cryptographic, and social curves to support a self-sustaining system. Most impressive is its ability to be exempted from the corruption we often see with centralized power.

Finally, we ended with examples of how it can be extended with alt-coins and how it can be used in various real world applications. The possibilities with Blockchain technology and how it can be adapted are truly endless. Although anyone can start a new alt-coin today, only those that bring true value to the market will succeed.

Today we have front-row seats to a historic transformation. Each one of us plays an active role in this transformation by our choices and actions; as a collective, we can shape the system to empower every individual. Presently, we have the power to improve conditions for economic globalization for us today, and tomorrow for future generations.

May the future of finance ultimately serve humanity and the planet it depends on!

www.ingramcontent.com/pod-product-compliance
Lightning Source LLC
Chambersburg PA
CBHW070314230526
45470CB00002B/878